KAY ATKINSON

How to start your own Food Tour business.

A beginner's guide to launching a food experience. Starting a side hustle and growing it into your dream job.

First edition

This book was professionally typeset on Reedsy.
Find out more at reedsy.com

To Jill and Louise who have supported me on my journey.
To all of our Food Ambassadors for being fantastic.

Contents

Introduction

What is a food tour?

A food tour is where a guide takes a group of people around a town or city and visits several eateries. In each venue, the guests will have a tasting of the offerings of that venue. The guide is there to talk them through the food, what it is and its significance to the local culture. Typically the guide also gives information about the venues, the stories of the people behind the venues and some history of the town or city, often seeing sights along the way.

It is a chance for visitors to experience the local area and is a great way for them to really get an insight into life there. They get to learn about the history of the place, some local stories and also about the cuisine. The cuisine can be a specialty of the area although that is not always necessary, it is about sampling the food scene of the area. For many people, myself included, it incorporates what many people like doing when they visit somewhere new; wandering around, finding out about the area without having to do lots of their own research on the internet and to have some great food. When visitors arrive in a town new to them they take a chance when picking a place to eat. Yes, there are Trip Advisor reviews but once you commit you have to have a whole meal and if you get it wrong, you feel cheated. On a Food Tour, the work has been done for you, your guide knows the best places to go and which dishes to try and if you like what you taste, you can go back for more! Saying that, Food Tours are also popular with locals as an interesting way to look at your home town with new eyes and discover new places. I have had people say to me on the tour "I've lived here 30 years and I never knew that" or "I never knew this was here" and we have introduced a new local haunt for them to frequent.

When I went to Chicago on holiday in 2011, I had never heard of a Food Tour. Determined to make the most of my week there, I had looked on the internet and had come across a Food Tour run by Chicago Food Planet. My friend David and I turned up at the appointed time and place and so began my food tour journey. Bruce was our guide and he was fantastic, keeping us entertained and in order and taking us on a culinary journey through the neighborhood. The details are hazy now in my memory but I remember a pastrami sandwich, fudge, olive oil, spices, pierogi and of course a stuffed pizza. It was exactly what I liked to do. I don't want to have to spend hours looking up places to eat and reading reviews or reading the history but I am interested in trying the local cuisine. It was the perfect way to spend an afternoon.

David and I were so impressed with the concept we immediately signed up for the Chicago Beer Town, also with Bruce and thoroughly enjoyed that too, although with alcohol it's a slightly different experience and I remember David getting a round of applause for being a card carrying member of CAMRA (Campaign for Real Ale). Incidentally, I met Bruce several years later in 2018 at the Food Tour Conference in Austin and was able to thank him for being an inspiration for my own Food Tour journey.

Catching up with Bruce

Back in my town of Harrogate in the North of England, I was inspired. Not only was Harrogate a Victorian spa town and a beautiful and popular place to visit, it also had a huge amount of fantastic cafes and restaurants and I knew a Food Tour would be a good addition. However, my children were younger at the time and I was teaching full time so it wasn't the right time. I had to console myself with just going on a Food Tour in every place I visited, a habit I have still not grown out of.

When I finally left teaching in 2016, I decided to take the plunge. I spoke to Shane Kost, the owner of Chicago Food Planet as I knew they ran a workshop for those who wanted to start a Food Tour. The only problem was there was not one in Europe, only in Chicago. That was my first leap of faith, I asked my sister if she fancied a week in Chicago, saved up a bit of money and booked myself in. It was invaluable in helping me. It provided a strategy to get to where I wanted to be and seven years later I have a great Food Tour business. It has taken time to build it up but I have really enjoyed the journey. Food Tourism and Food Tours have grown enormously as people seek more experiences than possessions and this book is to help you on your journey to running your own Food Tour business.

Your journey starts here by buying and reading this book. It takes you through the essentials of setting up your own Food Tour business. There is a lot of preparation to be done before you launch the tour but the speed at which you go is up to you. There are many great things about starting this business. You get to build something you can be really proud of, learn many skills and meet many great people on your journey. If you are interested in people and food, it is the business for you. You don't need much money to begin and it can be run with low overheads. It is ideal for building up beside your other responsibilities and then either going full time or keeping it as part of a portfolio lifestyle. Many of the topics we cover in the book are also useful for setting up any kind of food experience business, be it cookery classes or tasting events. The sky's the limit.

We have divided the book into the courses of a meal to keep that food flavor. Each of the chapters covers a key part of the journey to your own business. At the end of the 'meal' you will be full of energy for the journey ahead.

There are three main aspects which we cover:

- **Day to Day operation**. Having a clear set of systems to organize yourself and the business to ensure its smooth running.
- **Tour Experience.**The heart of the business. The Food Tour needs to provide the most enjoyable experience to the customer that you are capable of and offer good value for money.
- **Marketing.** A necessity. You need people to come on your tour so this covers how you reach and persuade those people.

The only thing you need is to take action. Even if it is a little action every day as it will build. Don't listen to naysayers who doubt you and keep going through the ups and downs. The reward is great. All our guides, myself included, find the tours themselves don't feel like 'work', it is just spending the afternoon with interesting people talking about food and life. So begin the journey and you will reap the rewards.

Chapter One. Preparation. The Business Basics.

Your Vision

It is worth spending a little time daydreaming before you start. Think about what you are wanting from this journey. Do you envisage it as a part-time business or becoming your entire financial and work life focus? You might be looking at your own town or a nearby city and see that is exactly what it needs if it has several great independents. Your area might have a speciality food that every visitor should try or some historical sights that are essential for every visitor to see. Give yourself permission to daydream. You might imagine yourself as a guide or as an entrepreneur leading the guides as they work for you. You might even have an idea of a name for your business or the places where you would like to go. Your reality may differ from your original daydream as you go through your journey but that doesn't matter, it is just a good starting point. I had the Chicago Food Tour as my inspiration. I wanted to show people my town and give them an insight into life in this little corner of Yorkshire. My town has a very famous tea shop who everyone who visits the town knows about. Very nice it is too but it is not the only place to get good food and Harrogate is an entrepreneurial town with lots of inspiring individuals who work hard to serve the visitors and locals. With the great rural North Yorkshire on our doorsteps, the local produce is abundant and this feeds the food businesses of the town. No longer is British food the poor relation of Europe.

Name and Identity

People often start with this. They become fixated on getting the brand name for their business just right and getting a logo. It is important but don't agonize over it. Give yourself a fixed time to decide and then just make a decision. There are many Food Tours around now so have a look at the names of those, you will soon see the themes that pop up time and time again. As you have these names, also check with domain providers to see if the domain name is available. You don't want to do all the hard work, make a decision then find out that someone else owns the domain for the name you want. After doing this, sit down and write down all those that come into your head. Keep that piece of paper with you for a week or so, ask the opinions of others that you value then a week later, sit back down and decide. Once you have decided, stick to that decision. Once you have your name, you will need a logo. At this stage though you don't have to wait until you have a definite logo. This work can be going on while you move on with your journey.

It is easy these days to make your own logo. It used to be the case that you had to find a graphic designer to work on it and with lots of to-ing and fro-ing it took time and often more money than you wanted to pay. Now there are logo makers on the internet. Many people are knowledgeable with IT and use programmes like Canva to make their own.

Type of Business.

This will of course depend on where you are situated. I am situated in the UK and here it is a case of deciding whether you want to be a Sole Trader or a Limited Company. There are pros and cons to each which you should consider. In the US, again the first thing you have to do is decide on a business structure. The four choices are Sole Proprietorship, Partnership, a Limited Liability Company or a Corporation. In the US, you need to register your business name. There are different ways to do this at both state and federal level. In the UK, this is not necessary although you can trademark your brand if you want but having the domain name is usually sufficient.

Financing your Business

This is a stumbling block for many people wanting to build a business. They think they don't have a large amount of money and therefore cannot start until they get this. The good thing about a Food Tour is that you don't need a huge amount of money. I cannot say you don't need any but you can start up with as little as a thousand pounds/two thousand dollars.

The key things to consider:

A business account. Do set up a business account and always keep things separate from your personal account. It will get messy if you are paying from one to another on a regular basis.

Start Up Capital. As I said, a small amount of capital is necessary to pay for the bare bones of the business. You will need a website, a domain name and running costs. Decide how much this is going to be. It depends how long you plan to prepare your tour before you are up and running but I would suggest one thousand pounds as a minimum. I took a loan of £5000 when I started, I put it in my business account and set up a standing order to pay back a hundred every month and then forgot about it. It pays off eventually and it is still there in that account. It is a tiny investment compared to many other businesses.

Cash flow. This is what this money in your business account is for. You will have expenses but soon you will have money coming in as tickets to your tour start selling.

Accounting.

Keep good accounts from the start. There are resources available to help you, such as books on accounting and simple bookkeeping. There are programmes available like Quickbooks and Sage which can help you keep track of finances. You can use a simple excel spreadsheet keeping a record of everything that goes out and in. It depends on your level of knowledge about accounting. Being organized is the key. Keep records, keep receipts. At the end of the year you will have to produce a set of accounts showing how much money you have made in order to declare it towards your income tax. If you don't have an accounting background, employ an accountant. It will be around a few hundred pounds well spent on your accounts. You may want to see one on a more regular basis if you feel you need to keep on top of it.

Tax

You will need to pay tax on what you earn from the business. That is why keeping a record of costs and revenue is essential. It is best practice to make sure you have money in your account to pay your taxes at the end of the year. Therefore keep an amount of money earmarked for tax. If you are going to draw an income from the business account each month, keep this in mind so that the tax money is not whittled down.

Remember – keep it separate from personal accounts.

Key Information

Ticket Price

This will be determined by your costs. You want to make enough profit to make it all worthwhile but you want to offer value for money. I have noticed in the last couple of years Food Tours have become much more expensive and sometimes it seems unreasonable if, for example, it is a street food tour and not a fine dining experience. Don't price yourself out of the market. Do some research on other food tour companies to see what they charge, how long they are and how many tastings they include.

Ticket Sales

It is best to sign up to a ticketing and booking platform. They are out there now and you can choose which ones. I use Fareharbor at present and find them very good. I did try to do it myself at one point but it is infinitely easier to use a service especially designed for this task. They are very good at offering a service including enabling people to book easily onto your tours, pay you regularly and make it easy to give refunds or discounts. Plus an addition I find hugely helpful is they have a support department which can help you if you get stuck. A lifesaver for those like me which have limited knowledge of technology. You will pay a small fee off each payment you receive but it is worth it for the trouble it will save you. You have to pay for a good service.

Guides

Many people when they start will be their only guide. In order to keep costs down, then this is the best way. It gives you an idea of what is involved, you get to know your tasting partners and it is important to have that hands-on knowledge of the product. We will be discussing using other guides later in the book.

Tasting Partners

These are your bread and butter. You cannot function without good tasting partners so it is essential to build good relationships with them. It may not always be easy and some will come and go but don't take it personally, the situation has to work for them as well so always be respectful and remember that they are a business too so work together.

Products

These are your tours. You may want to start with just one tour of your local area. It is a good idea to start with one and run it for several months before deciding whether to introduce another tour. This will give you an idea of the market and what works and what doesn't work. It takes a lot to develop a new different tour and you want to make sure it is worth it. There will be time for growth later, concentrate on getting started.

Financials

These are the key elements.

Revenue - this is money you make from ticket sales.

Fixed costs - this is money you pay out for costs that stay the same regardless of how many tickets you sell. For example, website, insurance, your operating costs and your marketing costs.

Variable costs - this is money you spend which varies depending on how many people are on the tour. These are essentially your food, guiding and ticketing costs.

To keep it very simple:

Fixed Costs + Variable Costs = Total Costs

Revenue - Total Costs = Profit.

It is helpful to have an idea of the amount of revenue you want to bring in each month so you have an idea of the amount of tickets you need to sell each month to achieve that.You can also work out how many tickets you need to sell to break even, so that every ticket over that number will make profit.

Chapter Two. Starter. Creating the Tour.

Researching Tasting Partners

"The perfect tour is like a carefully choreographed food ballet".
Shane Kost, CEO, Chicago Food Planet.

The first step is to draw up a list of possible tasting partners in the area of your town. If you are familiar with the area you will be able to put a fair few down straight off. Make a note of their name, their address and the type of food they serve. That's all you need to begin with. You can then try other sources to add to this list. Look at Trip Advisor for your town, Instagram and Facebook may add some more. Food blogs are also another source of information and ask around as to where local people recommend. There is always the walk around the town to see if there are any you are not familiar with.

Carry out some initial research into these venues. You need to know where they are obviously and also to have a familiarity with their menu in order to get an idea of what they could potentially offer as a tasting. Identify a short list of around ten venues that you are interested in.

Plan your route. Things to consider.

Distance.

How much walking will there be? We recommend between 1 and
1.5 miles. This will depend to a certain extent on your potential
market. You may have to consider people with mobility issues.

Walking.

Again, do consider if you have people with mobility issues. Does
the route include any steep hills? Are there any high pavements
or cobblestone roads to contend with?

Traffic.

Will you have to cross any main roads? Are they easy to cross?
Does the area get busy with people at various times? Are there
places to stand on the way which are not too noisy?

Time

How long is your food tour going to be? Most I find are around 3
hours long. It is hard to do a full tour in less than 2 hours and
some go up to 4. Tastings usually take about 20-30 minutes
so you need to bear in mind how long it takes to walk between
places and how long it will take to eat.

Between Tastings

You want to think about the route between tastings. It needs to be not too long, not too short and contain points of interest to help conversation and provide extra value to the tour. You want to get a good balance between tastings and walking in order to keep people's interest. Consider if you will have stops between tastings to look at sights. Make sure there is somewhere to stand where you are not obstructing others.

Weather.

Ah, the unpredictability of the weather. Of course, you may live somewhere with stable weather for which you can plan. I live in Yorkshire where the weather is definitely not consistent! They say 'if you don't like the weather, wait half an hour'. Tours need to take place come rain or shine so bear in mind on your route some good sheltering spots if necessary. You may want to provide umbrellas or ponchos but in my experience, if you warn people to come prepared for all weathers, they will.

Sitting or Standing.

You don't want to wear out your visitors. Whilst some tastings require them to stand, visitors always appreciate sitting at most places and particularly at the starting point especially if they may have to wait.

Starting and Finishing

We will discuss good starting and finishing spots later on but do consider at this point whether you would like a circular route or a one way route.

Facilities.

You need to be aware of the need for toilet breaks. Most places will have toilet facilities and it is useful to have at least one at the start, one at the end and one in the middle.

The Right Menu

The progression of the menu is key to a good tasting experience. It is always better to have larger or heavier tastings towards the beginning of the tour and then lighter ones towards the end. Visitors will have different appetites so some tastings towards the end could account for this. We find visitors like the traditional progression of a meal in terms of starting with savory before going onto sweet. I once went on a Food Tour which started with a beer tasting. I hadn't eaten much in preparation for the tour and so was rather squiffy from that moment on! It is not a good idea to switch from sweet to savory and back again.

Size of Group

Think about the minimum and maximum size of the group. Are you prepared to go with one or two people? What is the maximum number of people you want to take? At the beginning, we took one person but now we have a minimum of two people. I believe it is important to take tours even if there are few people. If you get into the habit of canceling if there is a minimum then you become unreliable and word gets around. Plus it takes time to build up your brand and popularity. The maximum will also depend on the size of the venues and how many they can accommodate. Also bear in mind the quality of the experience, if groups are too big the experience is less personal.

Number of Tastings

I have seen this vary a lot. Some tours have 4 good sized tastings whereas others will have 6 or 7 smaller tastings. It really depends on the time and the size of the tastings plus of course the cost. We have five on most of our tours but four on one.

Drinks.

This is a point of preference. I have been on tours where there is an alcoholic drink at nearly every stop (from what I remember) and those which have none. We always make sure water is available at each stop and include one small alcoholic drink (with non alcoholic alternative available). We have found that as we run daytime tours, about 50% of people don't want to drink. Many tours offer an upgrade to include alcohol or allow opportunities for people to purchase their own. It also depends on the food costs in your country, you will find in countries where wine is cheap for example, Spain and Portugal, it is often included but if you included alcohol in the UK or in the Scandinavian countries where alcohol is expensive then you are going to adding costs to your tour and will have to charge higher prices. The feedback we have had from the tours includes people who find there weren't enough drinks and those who think there are too many so it's a matter of choice. The vast majority are happy to pay to buy extra if they want them. If people don't drink they may feel they are not getting as much value.

Starting and Finishing Points

Some things to think about when choosing starting and finishing points:

Starting.

- · Is it sheltered from the weather?
- · Can they sit down while waiting?
- · Is there somewhere to get a drink if they arrive early?
- · Is it easy to find?
- · Can you arrive easily by public transport?

Finishing

- · Is it close to the starting point or public transport?
- · Are they able to linger if they would like?

Get yourself a map of the local area and make copies. To start with, highlight potential tasting stops and historical and cultural sights. Work out a few potential routes. Remember the menu must flow in logical progression. This will help you narrow down your tasting partner list. Once you have narrowed it down to those which might work for your route you are ready to draw up your short list. It is a good idea to have a short list as you can approach those potential tasting partners first and once you have your stops you can move on to the next stage. You might want to add more partners as alternatives (always useful to have extra in mind if anything happens to your original tasting partners) but this comes later. Then get out there in your town and walk the route. It helps you to see any potential issues, you can time the walk between stops and generally get a feel for the route.

The Pitch

Now you have your list of potential tasting partners, it is time to approach them. Prepare yourself. Decide how you are going to approach them and practice your pitch. Make sure you are knowledgeable about the place. Familiarize yourself with the menu so that you have an idea of what the tasting might be. Make sure the opening hours suit your tour.

I believe the best way to approach the tasting partners is in person. You can send an email but there is a high chance they will not respond. It is better if they see you and can put a face to the name. Choose a time when they are likely to be less busy, it is no good going in the middle of the lunchtime rush. Ask to speak to the manager or owner, explain who you are (a professional business card to hand out is helpful) and ask if they could spare 5 minutes to talk about possible involvement in your Food Tour. If they say they are busy, ask if you can come back at a more convenient time. They may sit down with you for 5 minutes or rearrange, if they ask you to email them instead then that is what you must do. If the owner/manager is not there, arrange to come back when they are and leave your business card.

You have that time to get them interested. Outline who you are and what you are developing. Be clear about what it would involve e.g. a small group coming every X day to have a taster and they would always know in advance how many were coming, what they would be eating and what time they would be there. In terms of price per head you can give them a rough idea of what you would like to pay and ask them what they could offer for that price.

Pricing

Before you approach them have an idea of the price you are willing to pay for your tastings. You want to be only spending 25% - 30% of your ticket price on food. Go in with the lower price in your head and then you have room to negotiate upwards if necessary.

After this initial conversation you should have an idea of whether they are potentially interested or not. Then you have to leave them to cogitate on the decision. After the meeting, follow up with more information. We have a sheet of information which covers the important points of being involved in the tour which we either leave with them to read over after the meeting or email to them. This information will answer every potential question they would have and address any obstacles that they may foresee.

These are some suggestions of what to include:

An assurance that there is no contract to sign and that either side can stop if they feel it isn't working for them in the future. Let them know the time scale in that it will take a short while for the tour to develop so it would not be an immediate start. Their biggest concern is usually that the tour will take up a table who are paying less money than usual customers. Remind them that stops are brief and you will be staying no longer than 20 - 25 minutes and they will always know when they are coming. Bear in mind if they have a preference for a particular time slot. Point out that most businesses see it as a marketing exercise as it showcases their food and often visitors will come back for a full meal at a later date.

Follow up and arrange another meeting to firm up tastings. Once you have the go ahead and tastings sorted from your necessary number of tasting partners you are ready to go.

This part, approaching the partners, was definitely the most difficult part for me when I first started. I was way out of my comfort zone but it is necessary and gets easier with practice. There will be some tasting partners who say no and cannot be persuaded. If they are negative on the first meeting then send or leave the information anyway and follow up with an email to see if they have reconsidered. If you get no reply, forget them and move onto the next alternative.

The Final Route

You have your tasting partners. You have your list of tastings. You know what historical and cultural sights you want to include. You can now map out your proposed final route. Walk it and time it. Just remember, it is never final, it can always be tweaked as you go on.

The script.

You will need to write a script for the tour. These are the things to include:

An introduction; who you are, where are you from and what they can expect from the tour. Check for any specific dietary requirements (you should have these from the booking already but some people forget!)

Information about the food. Where it comes from, what is its significance, why you chose it as a tasting, some history or interesting facts about the dish.

Information about your tasting partners. Their story. People like to hear about people passionate about their food business. Some partners will interact with your visitors or even talk to them which is great but obviously they are busy people so the tour guide must know the information.

History and information about the town and its sights. Research is necessary.

Once you have a script, learn it. You can adapt it as you go along and you will put your own voice on it and add bits in as you learn new things but this original script is your base.

The practice.

Walk through the tour yourself as you are learning the script. Organize that first tour for a small group of friends and ask them for feedback at the end.

You are ready to go.

Chapter Three. Main. Up and Running.

We will cover three areas in this chapter

- Sales
- Marketing
- Customer Service

Sales

You have the tour. This is your product. The first step is to be able to describe it well. You will need copy. Write a short description of the product, a mid length description and a really detailed description. This will get you ready. Photos are another consideration. When you are negotiating with your tasting partners ask if they mind if you use any of their photos on their website for marketing purposes. Take some photos of the food and the people on your practice tour. Remember you must only use photos you have taken or you have permission to use.

A website and domain name. This is essential. You can get this done for you by a professional website designer or you can do it yourself. When I first started, I got someone to design my website but it ended up that every time I needed to make changes I had to go through them and it cost me! In the end, I built my own. There are several platforms that enable you to do this. It takes time and is a steep learning curve (unless you are particularly technologically gifted) but it puts you in control. I am currently with IONOS and the good thing about using a platform is the support. If I don't know what to do I ring them up and they are available pretty much all the time and they talk me through it. It is a monthly cost but a necessary one. You won't be able to function without a website.

Most of these platforms also will manage your domains. Remember your domain name should be obvious and say what it is exactly. There is no point in having an obscure name because if they have just heard your name once, they need to be able to find you. For example, if your business is called Wentworth Food Tours, your domain should be wentworthfoodtours.com and not tastiestdishesintown.com.

Other things to consider when setting up a website:

- Colors and fonts. These should work well with each other.
- It should be a good representation of your brand.
- Your URL should clearly communicate who you are and work well in Search Engine Optimisation (people searching on google etc)
- Customers should be able to find information in two clicks.
- It should be clear how to buy tickets.
- It should work well across all devices; mobile and PC.
- You need to be able to update and maintain it easily.
- It should include key words. (key words are phrases that people type in the a search engine when looking for food

27

tours e.g. food tour, things to do).

- Include the following: : what a Food Tour is, how much it is, how many stops the tour has, where it takes place, how much walking it requires, what the price includes, the duration of the tour and your contact details.
- You need to link your website with your ticketing platform, Your ticketing platform e.g. fareharbor will be able to guide you through this.

Marketing - First steps

We will be discussing this later in the book in more detail but there are three key parts to marketing that you need to consider.

1. **Design.** This is your brand identity. You have your name, a logo, brand colors and an identity.
2. **Direct marketing**. This is your website, leaflets and email.
3. **Indirect marketing.** This includes you, content of marketing, public relations and SEO, search engine optimisation.

Customer Service

There are two sets of people you need to keep happy. Your customers and your tasting partners.

Your customers.

They are everything in this business. You must make sure they have the best experience you can provide from their first contact through to after the tour. Pretour they may have enquiries or difficulties with the booking process. It is a good idea to have a staffed contact telephone number. Make sure you respond quickly to their enquiries and offer alternatives if their first option isn't available.

During the tour, be mindful of their experience by reading the room. You may notice that some are walking slower than others or eating slower than others, you have to accommodate these things while keeping the group happy. You will sometimes get people who are rude or talk over you and you will learn strategies to deal with these as you go along. Most people are nice but problems and issues do occur and having a guide who can respond well to these is essential.

After the tour, follow up with an email asking them about their experience and giving them details on where they visited. Sometimes we send photos we took on the tour. No matter how good your product is, there will be occasional complaints or poorer reviews. Do not let these discourage you. People have their own ideas of what is good or not and sometimes their complaints are about things that you do not think should be changed. For example, someone complaining that they should have a choice of what they eat at each place (not the idea of a Food Tour) or that the price is too much (when you are competitively priced). The best thing is to read it and not respond right away. Take time to think about it, consider if what they said has any merit or could inform you on how to improve tours and to calm down. We always respond to any negative reviews politely and in as diplomatic a way as possible. Have a look at other Food Tours on Trip Advisor to see if they have any bad reviews and look at how they are answered.

Your Tasting Partners

You cannot run a tour without the support of your Tasting Partners so treat them well. The relationship has to work for both of you. You should always treat them and their staff with respect and consideration. That means not expecting freebies and understanding that they too are running a business. Their hosting of your tour should be easy for them to accommodate, you want to make your visit to them as easy as possible. Check in with the owners periodically so that there is an opportunity for both of you to review whether the relationship is working. Sometimes it may become clear that it isn't working for either party so you may decide to end the working relationship for whatever reason. Try to leave the door open to return and accept that things change. Don't take rejection personally. Building a good relationship is important and make sure you help them too by posting good things about them on social media and recommending them to people.

Chapter Four. Dessert. Day to Day Operations.

There are four parts to this chapter:

1. Admin
2. Accounts
3. Booking Procedures
4. Policies

Admin

There are a number of tasks which will need doing on a regular basis. Make a list of these and decide how often they need doing. The list below is a suggestion of the first few items, you will decide on your own list.

<u>Task How often</u>

Checking emails and triaging them into once a day which need dealing with today and those which can wait

Processing bookings once a day

Informing venues and guides of the week's weekly tour schedule

Update accounts weekly or monthly

Pay guides monthly

Content creation for social media monthly

Pay insurance Yearly

Accounts

We have talked already about the need to keep clear and regular accounts. You must keep a record of everything you spend and earn on the business. By doing it regularly, it keeps it up to date and enables you to see how the business is performing. Keep all receipts and invoices.

You can use accounting software, an accountant or a spreadsheet. If you are a limited company you will need to file accounts at the end of year with Companies House (in the UK). If you are a sole trader, you will need to fill in a self assessment tax return based on your year's accounts.

Booking procedures

Decide on the procedure for each of the following and stick to it. You can review it periodically as you may find better ways and systems to deal with these tasks.

- **Processing bookings.** This includes how you confirm them and whether you send reminder emails. Also what happens after the tour. You can work with your booking system provider to make these automatic.

  ·

- **Keeping track of enquiries.** Some companies have their own systems for this, others just answer them as they come in and do not keep records if no booking is made.

  ·

- **Maintaining a database of bookings**. Again, booking platforms will do this for you.

  ·

- **Having a calendar of tours taking place.**

  ·

- **How you contact your guides and inform them of the tours they will be guiding.**

Policies

These should have their own page on your website, usually with a link in the footer. You can write your own as there are many examples on the internet. You can also look at the policies of other companies and use them as a template and adapt them for your own use. It is particularly important to have policies regarding cancellations and refunds.

You will also need to have a privacy policy and data protection policy. You need to comply with rules about Data Protection which can be found online about how you use customer data. Some companies have sustainability policies.

Another policy you should have in place, though not on your website, is your insurance policy. You should take out public liability insurance for your tours. There are competitive quotes on the internet and some deal specifically with tour operators.

Chapter Five. Sides 1. Marketing.

The importance of having a marketing strategy

"Marketing is the management process responsible for identifying, anticipating and satisfying customer requirements profitably" (Chartered Institute of Marketing)

The 4 P's of marketing

Product

The product is your tour. You may have more than one product (more than one tour). You must make sure your product does what it is meant to do. It must meet expectations in order for it to achieve long term success. Consider how you can offer products superior to your competitors.

Price

Getting your price right is important. It must of course give you profit but also give value for money and sit right in the Food Tour market. See what your competitors are selling for. Consider who your market is and how much they would be willing to spend.

For example, students will pay less than older visitors.

Promotion

You want to develop the message you want to get out there and promote it in the best places possible (see place). It includes all the different methods you can use to increase sales.

Place

This is where you place your product for sale. You want to consider which media your market is likely to use for example what social media platforms they are likely to use or what publications they read.

Market Research

Who are your competitors?

It is worth it to see what other food tours and experiences are in your area so that you are informed when you are considering your product. Consider how you will make yours better. However it is important to remember not to be put off if there are several competitors, it shows there is a market. Be aware of competitors and what they offer but don't be discouraged in offering your own similar products. You don't believe Sainsburys or Walmart were put off opening a supermarket because there were already other supermarkets, do you?

Who is your customer?

Research how many visitors there are to your town and whether they are mostly domestic or international. This will help you build a profile of their characteristics in terms of gender, age range, origin, likes and interests and income. You will then be able to determine who you are marketing to and this will inform you the best method of marketing.

Set SMART objectives

1. *Specific.* Your objective should be direct, detailed and meaningful. For example: Increase sales by 20%. Bad example: To increase sales (too vague)
2. *Measurable.* Your objective should be quantifiable to track progress. For example:Increase website traffic by 70%. Bad example: Increase web traffic
3. *Achievable.* Your objective is realistic and you have the resources to reach it. For example: Increase sales on main tour by 15%. Bad example: Increase sales on all tours by 50% in the first six months.
4. *Relevant.* Your objective aligns with the goals of your business. For example: To introduce a second food tour. Bad example: To start offering walking tours.
5. *Time bound.* Your objective has a deadline. For example: Introduce second tour by January 202X. Bad example: Achieve growth.

Methods of Marketing

Website

This is your shop front. This is where people will come to see your products so we talked earlier about how you can set up a good website. There are lots of analytics you can use to see how it is performing such as Google analytics which shows you how many visitors you receive and how long they stay for. It can also show you which pages they visit and where they come from which means you could target places you get less referrals from. If you have a news or a blog section on your website, it updates the content and this makes google reread it and it will be pushed up the google ratings.

Leaflets

These are useful to put in tourist information centers, accommodation, food festivals, local cafes and on notice boards. Think carefully about what you put on it. For example, if you use specific times and places you have to change these as adaptations are made. Keep it simple but with enough detail to get them to look further on your website. It must be clear how they can find out more information. Find a local printer who is reliable and who can deliver quickly. They will often provide a design for you at a cost if you give them the text and the photos. Even if you have a reasonable design yourself, they need it in their own format. Make sure you get a copy of the files for the design so that If you decide to swap printers you have the files.

Email Marketing

Building up your email customer list is important but data protection means they must agree to this. There are various ways to do this. For example, you can have an option on the website to subscribe or if you use facebook ads for example, people can enter their email address to receive more information. You could run competitions where people use their email addresses however it must state somewhere that they may receive marketing and will have an option to unsubscribe. There are many programmes which will send mass emails. Mailchimp is an example of one and they will talk through how to do this. There are various levels of service, they often allow you to have a certain amount of addresses without paying before you have to upgrade.

Search Engine Optimisation (SEO)

Search engine optimization will help make your website more likely to be seen on google. There are various ways to do this and one of the main ones if getting keywords into your website.. This is a huge area which we will not be delving into here. There are SEO experts out there, many who say they are SEO experts and those people learning it themselves. One thing at a time.

PR – Public Relations

This is to raise your profile and get your brand known. You might want to stage an event or sponsor an event to get your name known. Sponsorship is very expensive though but being at local events, with branding on, does build awareness. Sometimes charities will ask you for a prize in return for promoting you but be selective and ask yourself if it will truly bring awareness. Business networking groups is also a way to get known locally and may help support you too.

Social Media

You need a presence and there are many ways to do this. Facebook, Instagram and X are the main ones. You could have a blog. You have to think about your market and which social media they are likely to use. You also of course need to be familiar with them and comfortable in how to use them. Sometimes it is better to do one really well than all of them badly. If you are a newbie then take it one step at a time. It is also very time consuming and you must decide how much time you are willing to spend on it. There are very good social media training courses out there on the internet or if you belong to a destination organization in your area, they may offer free training. Of course, you can pay someone to do it for you and this is what we do. I know my limitations in terms of time and interest in social media so decided to delegate this to the experts.

Third Party Sales

These are other companies who will sell your tours for you. There are many of these including the big hitters like Viator, Tripadvisor and Virgin Experience. They may or may not bring lots of sales and you can sign up with as many as you like but be careful of their terms and conditions. Be fully clear on how they will promote you, how they will pay you and what commission you will have to pay on their sales. In terms of commission the industry standard appears to be around 10-15%. Anything higher you have to look at your costs and see if you will still turn a profit. The big hitters often take a whopping 30%. You have to decide if the volume of sales is worth the big commission. Do keep a record of who you have agreed to sell through and their terms and conditions and review the number of sales you make through them on a regular basis.

Develop a marketing strategy

Once you have made your objectives clear, the next step is to decide what you need to do to meet them and then create an action plan. To make you accountable as to whether you are following your strategy, decide on a set date to review your objectives and if they are being met.

<u>**Example:**</u>

Objective: To grow ticket sales by 10%. Review Date: Monday 8th February 202X

Strategy 1: Increase social media presence of Facebook.

Action points

- Increase social media presence on Facebook
- Post three times a week on Facebook
- Invite others to like our page.

Strategy 2: Put on a Mother's Day promotion
Action points

- Source three pictures, write promotion copy and write a Facebook ad. Post ad for 25 days

Strategy 3: Offer an alcohol extension to the tour
Action points

- Work out the cost of the extension and how it would work
- Contact tasting partners to discuss alcohol addition to tasting.
- Write copy for the extension. Put on website

Strategy 4: Contact hotels in the town
Action points

- Write list of hotels in the town and decide on best way to approach them e.g. leaflets, in person, email

Chapter Six. Sides 2. Guides.

It is more than likely that to begin with you will be your only guide and it may be that you continue that way. However some will want to share the responsibility or expand so here we have some guidance on employing guides. It is an advantage to be your own guide for at least the first few months. You will come to know your product inside out and therefore be able to train the guides adequately. When it comes to taking on guides, the vast majority of food tour operators use freelancers where they pay them for the tours they take. There is a great deal of bureaucracy and legalities involved in legally employing guides and this will vary depending on the country in which you operate. Consider the advantages and disadvantages of employing guides or using freelancers.

Finding good guides can be challenging. Many use word of mouth but there are job sites you can use like Indeed or other platforms like Facebook. You do want to consider what the characteristics of a good guide are and what experience you require them to have.

Those characteristics involve the following:

- Experience of working with people and customers therefore having great communication skills.
- They need to be professional and reliable and have the ability to think on their feet and be able to solve problems calmly and effectively if they arise.

- They should be a clear speaker and be able to engage an audience. A strategy I have found useful for the second stage of an application process (after receiving a CV and a statement of interest in the position) is to ask them to send me a short video of them talking about their favorite dish or restaurant. If they are phased by this, they will not be suitable. When meeting them for an interview, I arrange to meet them at a particular landmark and then ask them to guide me to a suitable place for coffee and tell me why they have taken me there.

• ._

Training a tour guide

It is important that once you have recruited your guide you train them well. First of all, take them on a tour so that they see what they have to do. Once they have learned the script, they can co-lead with you and present some sections of the tour. Once they are ready, let them lead a tour with you on it to make sure you are happy with how they are performing. There is more than just the script to learn and below is what to include in their training.

- Ways to greet the customers and put them at ease.
- Where and how to stand when addressing the customers.
- How to keep the tour to time and in order.
- Awareness of volume including whether the customers can hear them and if the noise is too much on any part of the tour.

A guide is there not only to entertain and educate but to make your customers feel comfortable. The ability to small talk and interact and engage with people is hugely important. Being open and friendly will mean the customer will have a good experience and so a guide with a general interest in people is a must.

The guide is a representation of your company so you want a professional. They must look presentable, wear your uniform (if you have one) and focus on the job in hand. Occasionally using a mobile phone is necessary, for example if you have to contact a tasting partner at the last minute but otherwise, they should be out of sight.

In terms of gratuities, some customers will tip. It is up to the guide if they feel comfortable asking for tips and whether it will be at the beginning or end. This of course will depend on the custom of the country in which you are operating.

Look After your Tour Guides

Be well organized. You need to ensure the guide has the customer list and knows where and when their tours are. Have a good solid method of communicating the dates of the tours and a back up plan for any illness or unforeseen circumstances. Check in with your guide periodically by going on a tour or using a mystery shopper. Your reviews will inform you as well as to their performance. Sometimes things will go wrong or they may get a negative comment in a review. It is important to offer your support by discussing how to move forward from these issues. Finally, there is a tour script to follow but each guide may add little bits to put their own identity into a script so allow this.

There are some difficult situations that may come up during the tour so you need to come up with a strategy to deal with these and then discuss them with your guide as part of their training.

For example: what would you do in the following situations:

- Terrible weather.
- Customers questioning your historical facts or asking too many questions.
- Customers talking over you during the tour, not listening or using their mobile phone.
- Customers smoking.
- The staff of your venue not expecting you.
- The venue being closed when you arrive.
- Customers wanting to stop and buy something or wandering off to shop.
- Customers not liking the tasting.
- Customers not being able to eat the tasting due to an allergy they had not told you about.
- Customers injuring themselves or having an accident.
- Passersby tagging along as part of the tour or attaching themselves to listen to you.
- Unannounced guests arriving or wanting alternative tastings.

Chapter Seven. Coffee. Next Steps.

Set yourself a launch date and work towards it. This will give you the impetus to work forward to your goal so a plan of action each week is important. The biggest obstacle to businesses being a success is lack of action. If you feel you don't have time, make time. Set aside the required time each day, even if it is one or two hours only and make it sacrosanct to work on your business during that time. You will go through ups and downs of confidence and enthusiasm but the important thing is to keep moving towards that goal. At the beginning of the week, make an action plan with priority tasks at the top.

Short term goals.

Your first goal should be to launch your tour. Your second goal to review its progress after a month or two. At the end of six months or a year, have a review on how it has gone, what needs improvement and what is going well.

Long Term Goals.
You may have these in mind already and you can certainly put them in writing. Some may prefer to review them on a periodic basis. They will be based on where you want your business to go

in the future. Are you planning on introducing more tours and experiences? Do you want to build up the business to sell it? Do you want to grow your business or do you want to stay local and on the small scale. How much do you want to increase revenue.

Conclusion

Now you are ready. Be strong, be brave, take action. You can achieve your goals. If you would like help on your journey, then the Academy of Food Tour Operators can help you through support sessions. Have a look on our website or contact us directly. Once you are up and running, join our network so all of us food tour operators can support each other. I wish you the best of luck on your exciting journey.

www.yorkshireappetite.com

www.academyoffoodtouroperators

Drinks. Appendices.

Checklist
For each task, write yourself a deadline. Record the date you achieved it and make any necessary notes beside this.

Tasks

- Name and brand identity
- Website domain bought
- Register business
- Buy insurance
- Set up business account
- Accounting system
- Secure working capital
- Research potential partners
- Initial route
- Set initial ticket price
- Prepare to approach potential partners
- First approach to partners
- Follow up partners
- Final Route
- Script

- Write Copy
- Photos ready
- Website built
- Website hosting
- Terms and conditions and policies
- Time management procedure
- Booking procedure
- Marketing strategy and action plan
- Set up social media accounts
- Set launch date

Useful sites:
www.canva.com
www.fareharbor.com
www.ionos.com
www.ionos.co.uk
www.mailchimp.com

About the Author

Founder of Yorkshire Appetite Food Tours and the Academy of Food Tour Operators. Kay lives in Harrogate, North Yorkshire in the UK.

You can connect with me on:
- 🌐 https://www.yorkshireappetite.com
- 📘 https://www.facebook.com/yorkshireappetitefoodtours
- 🔗 https://www.instagram.com/yorkshireappetite
- 🔗 https://www.academyoffoodtouroperators.co.uk

www.ingramcontent.com/pod-product-compliance
Lightning Source LLC
Chambersburg PA
CBHW070439290526
45791CB00005B/2044